INTERNATI
How to g
the most effective step ~~by step guide for design students and graduates~~

"Ram is revealing what would take years to learn for students and graduates in one punchy, practical book."
– Matt Eastwood, *Worldwide Chief Creative Officer at JWT*

"As someone who struggled for two whole years to break in to my own creative career, I applaud Ram for sharing these vital tricks of the trade. I wish someone had been good enough to give me an insider's guide like this when I was starting out!"
– Ben Lilley, *Chairman and CEO at McCann Worldgroup*

"I congratulate Ram on an excellent guide for anyone aspiring to a career in design. It distills years of hard earned experience down into concise and practical advice on how to package, polish, promote and profit from your talent."
– Scott Smith, *Creative Director at RAPP*

"If you're serious about working in this industry, then read this book. Short, sharp and very real. It's an action guide. And it will provide excellent insight from the perspective of employers. It's partly poetic, and deeply informative."
– Andrew Hoyne, *Creative Director and Principal at Hoyne*

"A clear and concise step by step approach to getting a job in the design industry, Ram has compiled this engaging publication with hands on experience. The insights he gives are honest, refreshing and highly relevant to today's changing employment conditions."
– Ian Wingrove, *Creative Director at Wingrove Design*

"This book comes out of the gates swinging.
It's an eye opener for all design students and graduates
that are serious about choosing the path of design."
– Daniel Farrugia, *Design Director at Imagination*

"Selling yourself isn't an easy task.
The book 'How to get a job as a designer, guaranteed'
provides the priceless help you need to avoid bad interviews,
mistakes and disappointments."
– Marco Eychenne, *Executive Creative Director at Lavender*

"This is the missing advice they don't teach you in college
or university. It covers everything you need to know when
getting started and is a joy to read."
– Declan Mimnagh, *Creative Lead at Expedia (ANZ)*

"In my experience the lessons taught by failure and pain are the
most instructive. Ram shares lessons from his journey with a
healthy dose of both. Read, learn, enjoy the ride and launch your
career with a clearer sense of a path well followed."
– Ted Leonhardt, *Author: Nail It, Stories for Designers on Negotiating
with Confidence. Teacher: Creative Live, Worth It: Negotiation for Creatives.*

HOW TO GET A JOB AS A DESIGNER, GUARANTEED

THE MOST EFFECTIVE STEP-BY-STEP GUIDE
FOR DESIGN STUDENTS AND GRADUATES

RAM CASTILLO

Published in Australia by Ram Castillo in 2014

Cover and book design: Ram Castillo

Editor: Melissa-Jane Fogarty from MJ Editing

Typesetting and publishing assistance by Publicious
www.publicious.com.au

For general information or enquiries, please contact Ram Castillo
via email: ram@giantthinkers.com

More information can be found on www.getajobasadesigner.com
and www.giantthinkers.com

*For my parents Romulo and Luningning Castillo,
whose light shines brighter than a world where deferred
dreams are the norm. I am the product of your love
and am infinitely grateful.*

CONTENTS

—

WE ACCEPT THE LIFE
WE THINK WE DESERVE.

—

INTRODUCTION

WHY YOU NEED TO READ THIS BOOK

This book will serve one main purpose:

To reveal to you my proven strategy for the most effective and practical way to get a job as a designer (graphic, print, web, digital, environmental, experiential, UX/UI, 3D and motion) in the industry, guaranteed.

There are only five specific parts you need to develop well in order to get a job as a designer. Attacking the steps outlined in this book will be the difference between you wishing you were a designer and you actually earning a more than comfortable income as one. The quality in which you execute these five parts will dictate the quality of employment and more importantly the lifestyle you will live.

The five parts in order are:
Education
Design
Portfolio
Networking
Interviews

WHO THIS BOOK IS FOR

If you're a design student or design graduate, this book will lead you to doors you never thought existed. After reading this, my hope would be for you to walk away with any myths or barriers diminished and replaced with a clear action plan. Allow it to ignite your mind to the reality (not just the idea) of abundant opportunities. Stop putting your dream on an unreachable pedestal. Park any negativity or hesitation aside, even if only for the duration of this book. You can pick up those doubts, fears and thoughts of skepticism at the end of the book if you'd really like to return to them. For now, I ask you to be open to new thinking.

For the purpose of setting parameters for this book, let me clarify, this isn't about how to be successful or happy. Both of those areas are only measured by your personal philosophies on the purpose of life. There are many other resources out there about those topics, which you can investigate. There are far too many variable and complex influences such as culture and upbringing that can take more than a lifetime to discover and yet you may still not find any clarity on those subjects. If however you believe that working and living a life in the design industry will be fulfilling, and act as a vehicle contributing to your reality of success and happiness, then you will find practical answers here to achieve that quickly.

Those of you who have decided on a career change and have specifically made an upfront commitment to become a designer will also benefit. On top of that, current designers struggling to get employed should use this to review their approaches.

THE THREE BIGGEST FEARS THAT STOP PEOPLE FROM BECOMING DESIGNERS

1. I'm scared that when I finish my course, I won't get a job because the competition will be too high.

2. I don't think I'm as creatively talented as others, I can't even draw.

3. I'm too old to start learning about design, it's too late.

These are some common limiting beliefs we may all go through. So before you self sabotage your progress, let me tell you, it can be done. You can work as a designer and earn as much as you're committed to making. How do I know this? Because I've done it. And I've written this book as if it is addressed to my younger self: *Why didn't anyone tell me what I know now, sooner?*

Whatever your fears are, they're no different from the fears felt by the next person. You and I are no different to world leaders, great innovators and successful entrepreneurs. We all have a beating heart, we have flaws, weaknesses and make mistakes. However, we also all have choice and the ability to decide how to respond to what life throws at us. We can see a glass half full or a glass half empty. We can see a setback as a huge struggle and give up, or we can embrace it and enjoy the learning, motivated by the fact that setbacks are necessary for growth.

All that you have in your life at this very moment began with nothing but a thought. Then you took massive action and the necessary steps to reach those goals. Everything you want is on the other side of fear. Aim high. Take ownership of your life and fight for it. We're only passing through this world once, make it count.

—

IF YOU WANT TO INCREASE YOUR SUCCESS RATE, DOUBLE YOUR FAILURE RATE.

– THOMAS J. WATSON

—

—

WHAT ARE YOU GOING TO DO TODAY WITH YOUR ONE AND ONLY LIFE?

— RAM CASTILLO

—

MY STORY

My story begins before me.

She was the third child of five siblings, raised by a strong-willed mother and a father who for the most part provided from a distance. Her food for the day was usually a small piece of bread and if lucky, a tablespoon of soy sauce. Constantly sick, this became the usual. Growing up in the Philippines in the 1960s and 1970s was tough to say the least, but she knew nothing different.

All her riches lay within her desire and perseverance for continuous learning and hard work. That key eventually opened the door to a world of opportunity. From winning full scholarships, to teaching students, to working for one of the biggest banks in the world, the path she paved is a journey that keeps me grounded.

This woman, is my mother.

My father was the eldest of three direct siblings as well as, four half brothers and five half sisters. When my father was only three years old his father passed away and he quickly had to learn the ropes of provider. He would wake up at five am every day to help his mother at the markets before school.

He was short in height from carrying heavy bags of rice daily, but his heart could sell out a stadium. Motivated by desperation, he committed himself to a better life despite the odds.

From being a certified black belt champion, winning multiple National Karate tournaments in the Philippines, to owning a local restaurant and even graduating with a double Bachelor's Degree in Marine Transportation and Mechanical Engineering, this man proves that success is a decision.

I was fortunate enough to open my eyes to this world on the 23rd of April 1986. My family migrated to Sydney, Australia from Manila when I was eight months old. If I could sum up my life as a child in one word, it would be 'active'. Most of the time you'd find me climbing trees, running around with a soccer ball, riding my pushbike or eating Nutella sandwiches. At other times I was enjoying collecting scraps such as empty tissue boxes and toilet paper rolls to build robots. I had a very curious mind but didn't feel it was hugely different to the curiosity of most children.

I can easily list a hundred life-defining moments. They all taught me priceless lessons that I could never have learnt from a book or a video. Rather than explaining to you about each one, I'd like to share with you a mixed bag and have you interpret them for yourself.

1. **I broke my arm three different times and had a total of 16 stitches all before the age of 11.**

I learnt about self-awareness and physical pain. I also discovered that we aren't invincible and that we don't need to touch fire to know it's hot!

2. **I was denied by exactly 99 design and advertising agencies in grade ten for work experience.**

As part of the curriculum we had to organise work experience on our own by contacting any company of our choice in any industry that interested us. When I was just about to give up, it was the 100th call that did it. I was 15 years old and the first person that gave me a chance in the design industry was Ian Wingrove, Creative Director and Founder of Wingrove Design.

We kept in touch and five years later I received a timely call to meet with him to work on a pitch for his agency. We won it and I stayed on board for three years. I learnt the impact of perseverance and keeping in touch. Somewhere, someone will give you a chance. Keep going. The right opportunities will present themselves to those that want it bad enough.

3. I accepted the end of a long-term relationship and went backpacking for five months around Europe on my own.

I learnt that when you ask for something, the answer may not be what you want at the time and certainly not what you expect. During this time of self-discovery, I felt a different type of pain.

Not realising at the time, but it was like a sculptor using a hammer and chisel for its subject matter as he chipped away unnecessary pieces in order to create a masterpiece. The process hurts but is required for growth and value.

Oftentimes, what we associate as a huge heartbreak or disappointment, is actually the springboard to a better, more fruitful and liberating life. It's astounding how perspective can be just a plane ride away.

Something in particular happened during this trip, something magical and memorable, which I'll reveal to you later on.

4. Being the recipient of a scholarship and starting early didn't guarantee me a job in the design industry.

I was privileged to have a calling to art and design at a young age and even win a full scholarship at a design college.

This didn't dismiss the fact that I needed to work hard. Really hard. In fact, I started in the mailroom of Singleton Ogilvy & Mather, Sydney when I graduated. Delivering mail, newspapers, dispatching packages and ordering toner for four floors containing 350 employees.

I learnt early on in my career that you have to demonstrate your abilities beyond the paper you've earned. Graduating in design doesn't give you a golden ticket to a job. I discovered that sometimes you need to take a side step in order to take a forward step. That getting your foot in the door first is a wise strategy for the long-term as you expand your network and become exposed to established creative thinkers and doers.

YOUR STORY

Like you, we all have a story to tell and more importantly a story to create. If I may ask you ever so bluntly, why do you really want to be a designer? Ask yourself honestly, now and often. Be clear about your reason. Your reason should have some weight. Put things that truly matter on the line.

The aim is for your reason to be powerful enough to carry you through times of struggle and doubt. Nothing worth having comes easy. Any successful person can tell you that great achievement doesn't come without a fight and it doesn't happen overnight. It takes vision, unwavering commitment, patience and consistent action.

The ability to be louder than loud without ever making a sound is why I chose the path of design. To create an emotional connection through a single visual idea and to influence human behaviour was the seed that fascinated me.

Now, it's become far more than that. Design has become a complete lifestyle. It's the vehicle that allows me (and many of my peers) to live with imagination, optimism, positivity, humour, adventure and freedom. I've been able to experience an abundance of intellectual, emotional and financial wealth and share that with the people I love far beyond what I ever dreamed. If you had asked me when I was 18 years old that sorting mail, stocking paper, toner and drink fridges would lead me to a life this fulfilling, you would've been my favourite comedian.

So dream big.

As has been said many times before:

If your dreams don't scare you, they aren't big enough.
– Ellen Johnson Sirleaf

—

Your work is going to fill a huge part of your life and the only way to be truly satisfied is to do what you believe is great work. And the only way to do great work is to love what you do. If you haven't found it yet, keep looking. Don't settle.

… I have looked in the mirror every morning and asked myself: "If today were the last day of my life, would I want to do what I am about to do today?" And whenever the answer has been "No" for too many days in a row, I know I need to change something.

… have the courage to follow your heart and intuition. They somehow already know what you truly want to become. Everything else is secondary.

— Steve Jobs, Stanford Commencement Speech, 2005

—

PART 1: EDUCATION

DO I NEED A DEGREE TO 'GET INTO' DESIGN?

This may come as a shock to you so take a deep breath and cover your ears. No, you do not need a degree to become a Designer. Did Michael Jackson need a degree to sing? If you have a calling to design, then don't let a piece of paper stop you. You don't need permission to start. Work with what you've got and proceed from there. To those in the boat of, "but I can't afford to start," I say, "you can't afford not to start". Regret is ultimately far more costly and painful than trying. If getting a job as a designer matters to you, then you'll find a way. If it's not, you'll find an excuse.

THEN DO I NEED A DIPLOMA OR CERTIFICATE IN DESIGN TO WORK AS A DESIGNER?

No. If we're strictly speaking about absolute employment mandatories, technically you don't need any kind of formal qualifications in order to work in the design industry. If you're a self-starter you can teach yourself or be guided by online tutorials. If this style of learning is more effective than being in a classroom, don't fight it. Ride that wave. This path would suit those who lack time and money. Read books on design principles, follow online tutorial exercises, watch videos and have a play on relevant programs. This can all be done in your own time outside of your current full-time job and other responsibilities. The goal is to eventually have a few foundation pieces as your portfolio, even if they are based on 'dummy' briefs.

BUT THERE ARE DESIGN JOBS ADVERTISED THAT STATE THAT TERTIARY EDUCATION COMPLETION IS A MUST?

There will be some instances where completing a Diploma of Graphic Design or a Bachelor of Design will be favoured of course. However, there are always opportunities where employers take more consideration to previous work experience, work ethics, attitude, passion and natural talent.

IS THERE A 'BUT' IN THERE SOMEWHERE?

Just because tertiary education isn't mandatory to becoming a successful and employable designer, it doesn't mean I don't recommend it. In one way or another, you need to learn about design thinking, design principles and design execution. The vehicle you choose to learn from is completely your decision. Asking yourself questions such as: "What will make me a better designer in the shortest amount of time?" or "Which learning path will I enjoy the most and will give me the best opportunities?" will all help you to make the right decision. There is no single 'cookie-cutter' approach to having a high level of design competence.

Needless to say, everyone has different characteristics, financial circumstances, networks, learning preferences and objectives. Some of you may prefer to study a four-year degree, some a one-year diploma course, and others to be immediately on the job even simply as a part of the administration staff with exposure to creative thinkers and doers.

There are plenty of world-renowned Creative Directors, leaders and award-winning Designers who have pursued the path of design and the business of communication successfully with and without formal education. Some like David Ogilvy (known as 'The Father of Advertising') who was hands-on straight after secondary school. He started as an apprentice chef, then moved on to selling cooking stoves door to door and that lead him to a job in Mather & Crowther where his career truly began. Others like Vince Frost graduated from a Bachelors degree, and then started at

Pentagram in London, UK. Eventually he built his own studio which has lead him to the role of CEO of his new business structure, Frost* Collective based in Sydney, Australia. Frost has been a creative powerhouse of cutting edge design for the last decade.

You should never feel forced to do something you're not comfortable with. Some people prefer the face-to-face disciplinary learning of University structuring and the conceptual modules it brings. Others prefer the hands-on tools approach to learning in a private design college environment. And some would much rather teach themselves and start from the bottom in any entry-level position. These people learn on the job even if it isn't 100% directly related (such as starting as a receptionist or working in the mailroom in an advertising agency or design studio). By getting your foot in the door, you're immediately exposed to real projects. Even if you do start in the mailroom like I did (yep, I was a paper pusher) you're surrounded by 'live' jobs. Overhearing creative conversations, seeing work in progress and visuals stuck on walls are only some of the benefits. The truly invaluable part is making industry contacts and networking with influential Directors.

WHERE YOU CAN START

Assuming you commit to a design course or degree, let's first talk about getting professional experience while studying. The best way to beef up your resume and to earn some professional 'street cred' is to take on internships (paid or unpaid). Many times these internships are unpaid for course credit. Your 'Career Services' office can help you qualify for an internship or simply contact as many design studios or creative agencies directly, to open the conversation. Ask them, "What are the steps I need to take to come in for some work experience?" and go from there.

Taking on internships while studying shows a potential employer three things:

1. You know how to manage your time with school and an internship.
2. You take initiative in improving your educational and professional development.
3. You're passionate.

These are three great qualities to have coming out of the gate. On top of that, internships aren't only primarily for hands-on experience. Equally as important (if not more so) is the exposure to career mentors and meeting industry creatives who have large professional networks that they can refer you to in the future.

NOTE: If you decide to teach yourself using online resources available to you, the very first step is to learn the tools (Adobe Illustrator, InDesign and Photoshop are the most common foundation programs). Once you're competent enough, over time you'll be able to bring your ideas and design solutions to fruition. The next chapter will expand on this further and the end of the book has a resources list that will help you get started.

HARD WORK WILL ALWAYS BEAT TALENT WHEN TALENT FAILS TO WORK HARD.

— KEVIN DURANT

PART 2: DESIGN

DESIGN DOING

No matter what educational path you've chosen, start designing. Whether they're assignments, personal projects, real briefs or even dummy briefs, you need to start designing work so you can begin to think conceptually and learn to use the tools and programs. Your learning will be a continuous journey no matter what stage you're at.

Find a mentor to guide you through this period and give you experienced feedback and constructive advice on improving. Aim high too. You'll be surprised how generous creative leaders can be if you just ask with sincerity and humility.

DESIGN TIPS TO TAKE TO YOUR GRAVE

You will either cover these in your design fundamentals modules if you decide to study in a course or you will no doubt encounter this on the job. You'll face these points again and again in your career, and it only reaffirms their importance.

In my experience, the most important areas to consider when designing are:

1. Relevance

Do not be led by aesthetics. I'll say it again. Do not be led by aesthetics. Be led by relevance. I cannot emphasise this point enough. This requires you to do adequate research before beginning any design brief. The more you know about your communication objectives, the target audience demographic, the culture of the brand, the perceptions of the market and the environment the design will be seen in, the clearer your mind will be when making design decisions.

Once you start uncovering this information, you can get to the solution quicker because you're informed by the psychology of the people you are speaking to. In your attempts to create disruption, always ask yourself, "Does it create relevant cut through and relevant conversations between brand and consumer?" Oftentimes relevance is what creates the disruption you're looking for.

2. Having a grid system

Whether you stay in the grid or break out of it, you must have one. Why? Because you need to organise the information in a hierarchy that is easily digestible, alluring and pleasant to look at. Do not start a thing without one. Four columns, six columns, 12 columns – see what works best for the brief or task.

3. Hierarchy

Ask yourself, "What is the one thing I am trying to say?" That single, primary message must be the focus and must be unmistakably clear.

The secondary message should then substantiate the initial claim or idea, usually through transparent and honest proof points. For businesses, this substantiation strengthens their brand values on top of acquiring new customers and retaining existing ones.

The third should present a call to action (abbreviated as 'CTA') to the audience. Get them to do what it is you want them to do. Whether it be clicking a button, turning a page, buying the item, calling a number, interacting with it or sharing the content. Whatever it is, you've gotten their attention, you've raised awareness and led them to do something. Don't make them work hard for the message.

A clear hierarchy of information will help achieve an engaging and memorable customer experience. It's also worth noting that each touch point will likely have a different message. This ties in with brand strategy, but as an example, outdoor and print advertising may just be a teaser and direct the audience to the online space. From there, a landing page may hold a competition which leverages social media marketing, and participants are then engaged further via email and then to an event in a month's time. As you can imagine, these different touch points have different conversations but are overall defined by a customer experience structured by hierarchy.

4. Typography

Typography can make or break any communication piece. It's a craft in itself. Kerning and leading text should become second nature and used appropriately. Your objective should be on legibility first and foremost. So if the heading or copy needs more space then give it some, if it needs to be tighter then make it tighter. Font weights and size should be used in consideration with information hierarchy.

For example, using a bolder weight for sub-headings and a lighter weight for copy is common as it helps the reader scan the content of the page easily. Line breaks must flow both with the reader's eye and with the content. A line break shouldn't be disruptive.

Typography overall need not be flat. You're only restricted by your imagination. For instance, if you're designing a poster with the word 'SUMMER', there's no reason why you shouldn't explore the letters with beach-themed objects. If it hits the tone of the brief then great, if it doesn't, it'll reaffirm that the other design direction you've done is the better solution.

5. A single-minded message

Does your design enhance the message? Is it original in a way that communicates a different solution to a real problem? Is it clear and uncluttered? This level of intelligence is the 'wow factor' Creative Directors are looking for. Don't be fooled, cleverness is often frighteningly simple.

6. Creativity

If you can implement the above points, you've got the foundation of a good design, but that's only 50% of it. A truly great design injects the above fundamentals with a big idea. A big idea is the springboard into relevant and multi-layered conversations. Conversations that are compelling enough to effortlessly guide the customer on a journey that informs and engages them to take action. A creative spark that's simple and immediate. You'll know you've done this when you've captured attention, created delight and delivered meaning.

Think broadly. Your big idea should be a continuous story that lives on all relevant touch points.

—

Never walk into a briefing thinking you know the answer.
Dig deep into the briefing, ask loads of questions.
Immerse yourself in the organisation or the problem.
Discover a strong understanding.

Once you have done that, Brainstorm ideas quickly.
Play with it. Let your mind wander. Think lateral.
Involve your clients in the process.
Be transparent, collaborate.
Lead the outcome but don't dictate it.
Bring the best, 'the one', to life.

Remember it's not about you.
You're not an artist you're a service.

— Vince Frost, CEO and Executive Creative Director,
Frost* Collective

—

PART 3: PORTFOLIO

WHAT IS A PORTFOLIO?

A portfolio is a refined and considered selection of your best work, customised to speak to the area of design you are applying for. It should showcase your proven abilities, examples of completed work and potential for growth. Let's break this down:

DEFINE WHO YOU ARE SPEAKING TO

Your portfolio of work should directly translate to the role you are applying for. There's no point putting a tonne of packaging design and print brochures into your portfolio and then applying for a junior digital designer role, especially when they've specified that the duties include: UI/UX Design, wireframes, eDMs and landing pages.

Design to what you are truly passionate about.
I can't emphasise this enough.

As a side note: I do believe that digital designers and creative technologists (in the space of web/online, UX/UI, apps, 3D, animation and motion graphics) will continue to be in greater demand than print designers and therefore have more opportunities.

However, if you're absolutely stuck on print design, there will always be a place for it. Consumers will still buy bottles of milk, boxes of pizza and jars of peanut butter. We as humans will still appreciate and react to a beautifully designed book, magazine or way-finding signage, and will always notice a traffic stopping billboard ad. These things won't be disappearing anytime soon. So design to what you love and if you don't know how, then up-skill. There are plenty of free tutorial articles and videos online to assist you. Checkout: design.tutsplus.com and lynda.com as a starting point. There's also additional listed resources at the very end of this book.

HOT TIP: To create an even more impressive portfolio, include work beyond the same University or College briefs seen again and again. Invent your own brief. Or even better, do pro-bono work for a charity. By doing this, your work is live and the employer can see the tangible effect and outcome of your efforts. It will show passion, and the ability to go above and beyond.

Print design versus digital. Usually print design becomes the common foundation for most designers and a transition is gradually made to digital. The basic design principles are the same. Considered hierarchy, well-crafted typography and grid systems are all part of the design process no matter what discipline.

What you really need to hone in on is the tools, and designing to the behaviour of the customer and their device. Each device has a different customer experience just like the design of a Snickers bar sold at a 7 Eleven is different to the design of a chocolate bar sold at a Lindt Cafe. The store environment, the lighting and the customers are from two different ends of the spectrum. The same with viewing a website on a desktop that differs to viewing it on a smart phone. The versions must be responsive and change to cater for the digestion of information the device will allow. Even if you do stick with print design, you'll still benefit from additional digital knowledge because your ideas can be transferable on any platform. Don't be afraid of digital. Embrace it if you haven't already. You'll add a whole new dimension to your own personal brand and it is an important part of the customer experience.

INCLUDE IMAGES OF YOUR WORK

I recommend photographing your work wherever possible for one main reason; it looks like a real, live job and adds more substance to your portfolio. Even if it isn't a project based on a paid client brief, a photograph of the mock-ups will bring your work to life and make it more tangible. There's nothing worse than seeing an image of the flat artwork especially with printed pieces. I've even seen some with crop marks included. No points earned for attention to detail there. Even if it's a website, try to render it in perspective within a desktop screen, iPad or smartphone, or all of these. Ideally, either photograph the printed pieces or render them in their environments.

Common examples in your portfolio can include taking photos of:

- Identity and branding applications (logos, letterheads, business cards, envelopes, pens, USB sticks, bags, coffee cups, t-shirts, cars, badges and items relevant to the business) in a mix of close up shots and arranged in a neat group to extend the identity

- A printed poster

- A series of publication layout spreads (showcasing your typography ability)

- A rendered billboard or bus shelter poster

- A rendered website on an iPad and/or smart phone device

HOT TIP: Take a look at online portfolio examples at theloop. com.au/portfolios, filter the profession category and choose the 'popular' tab and you'll get a good idea of the level required.

TYPES OF PORTFOLIOS

How you present your work is as equally important as the work itself, if not more. Take Justin Gignac for example from nycgarbage.com. A New York City based artist and entrepreneur who began selling garbage in 2001 after a co-worker challenged the importance of package design. To prove them wrong, he set out to find something that no one would ever buy, and package it to sell. Looking around the dirty streets of Times Square, garbage was the perfect answer. 13 years later, over 1,400 NYC Garbage Cubes have been sold and live in 30 countries around the world.

Now I'm not saying design rubbish and only focus your energy on how that is presented. What I do advise is that you consider how the work is housed because it will either help your work shine or be its downfall.

Your work should ideally speak for itself, in which case, you should keep the portfolio clean, organised and minimal in its captions.

The main portfolio platform you should have is an online website. Having a printed portfolio and an emailable PDF portfolio is outdated. Your website should be responsive and can be presented on a laptop or iPad during face-to-face interviews, making a printed portfolio obsolete. Emailable PDFs can also sometimes bounce back and not go through to the person you're sending it to. The file may be too big for their inbox. On top of that the PDF may lose visual quality. Emailing the URL link of your online portfolio website will have a higher viewing rate due to its easy access.

HOT TIP: One huge bonus of having a website is the ability to add videos. Case studies on projects or hype reels are highly engaging to showcase a project or campaign. They don't need to be long or overly complicated either. Imagine showing your identity design in motion within 30 seconds and showcasing a few branding elements coming to life. Add that with the appropriate music and you've not only got a powerful story but content that is likely to be shared online.

CREATING AN ONLINE PORTFOLIO

Keep it super simple. The less clicks the viewer has to make to view your work, the better. Check out mine at ramcastillo.com but there are thousands of portfolio sites out there. Compare yourself with the best and never compare yourself with the worst. Find sites you like; assess the navigation, look at how they're organised and create your own.

A quick and very cheap option to get you off the ground is to customise an existing WordPress template that you like. There are thousands of different templates out there. There's nothing wrong with using a template site as a foundation to showcase your portfolio pieces because it's just a container. Your time and energy should go into what's inside it. One of the most popular collections can be found at themeforest. net. Also check out squarespace.com which has exceptional responsive website templates at a small ongoing cost with a custom domain name, hosting and extras all in one.

Wherever you find it, make sure your template:

• Is pre-coded as mobile responsive

• Has a user-friendly curating system

• Has large real estate for viewing images

• Has easy colour palette customisation

• Has well-positioned social media sharing integration

• Has a space for your logo in the top header

There are also many free portfolio sites. At least have an online presence on theloop.com.au, behance.net, cargocollective.com or coroflot.com.

Start somewhere. But start. Don't wait for things to be perfect before you do. It'll never be perfect and therefore you'll never get anywhere. Do what you can and improve as you go by launching a portfolio website that shows even a few of the designs that represent you accurately. The goal of your portfolio is to ultimately create enough interest and intrigue for an employer to contact you for an interview. If they at least get a snapshot of your abilities and see a spark of brilliance, whether it be from your design execution or your clever ideas, then your portfolio has done its job.

CAPTIONING YOUR WORK

I suggest having minimal captioning of your work with only the most necessary information to avoid overshadowing your work with too much text. This will allow the work to speak for itself as much as possible. What to include:

- **Client** – you need to name who the work is for.

- **Agency** – name the company or studio you did the work at. If it's a piece you're showing that's from college, university or school, then leave this label out and mention it in the next blurb (the 'Challenge' caption).

- **Challenge** – tell the viewer in a sentence or two what the primary objective was. What was the business problem or task? This will give the viewer background and put your designs into context. For example: "The objective of this mock-up brief was to re-brand a clothing label that we felt could be improved. The scope of work had to include new designs of their logo, stationery, clothing tags and website home page."

- **Role** – in reality, most projects have multiple people involved. This is an important opportunity to be transparent on what you are capable of and in a way, indirectly shows what areas you can improve on. If you have created your work from 'concept to finished art' then say so. If you were only responsible for, for example: "Design while working collaboratively with Creative Director Billy Bob and image retouching by John Smith" then that's cool too. As long as you're honest and upfront as this will form expectations around you, show your integrity in the work and the people that helped bring it to life. You don't want to get embarrassed showcasing a piece of work that they've already seen as you attempt to claim it 100% as your own. The strongest relationships are based on trust and honesty. In business, those values are no less true. The unspoken rule is to credit others when necessary and you too shall be credited!

CREATE AN EMAILABLE PDF RESUME WITH YOUR PORTFOLIO URL

Although having an emailable PDF portfolio is outdated as mentioned above, it is still important to have an emailable PDF for your resume, which is fine to send out because the file size will be significantly smaller than that of your portfolio.

Your resume PDF will act as an easy to access overview of who you are, what you've done, what you're doing now and what you aim to do in the future. You should also have your LinkedIn profile completed as much as possible. You can take the information you use below to replicate it onto your LinkedIn page. I'll tackle more about LinkedIn in a later chapter.

The structure for your emailable resume PDF should be as follows:

1. Your name, job title and contact details including your online portfolio URL.

2. A three-four sentence introductory blurb on who you are and the specific role you're looking for (literally spell it out, it's important to be very clear at the beginning). You can even mention what you're passionate about to add a personal touch.

3. List your employment history. Ideally this would all be relevant to the job you're applying for, but if you've never had a design job before, I'd suggest you put any type of work you've done in the past; internships, unpaid work placement or volunteer work. Each place you list should have the name of the company or organisation, the date you were there (month/year), duration and a sentence or two on what type of tasks and responsibilities you had with them.

4. List your education and qualifications history from high school upwards and any relevant courses, workshops or seminars you've attended. This fourth section can come before the third section ('list your employment history') if you have had minimal employment history.

5. List the key programs, software and platforms you know how to use. This would usually include at the very least, Adobe Photoshop, InDesign, Illustrator and Microsoft Office. You may or may not want to label next to each

whether you are highly proficient in them or not. But I'd suggest if you aren't, then don't label them. At the end of the day, you will continue to learn about these programs no matter how much experience you have. It'll be a given that your experience will reflect your proficiency.

6. List five-ten of your demonstrated design abilities, for example:

- Sketching and story boarding

- Idea and concept creation

- Corporate identity

- Magazine layouts

- Typesetting and formatting

- Environmental graphics

- eDMs

- Responsive websites

- Image retouching

- Finished art

7. List five-ten of your personal strengths and core values, for example:

- Open-minded and optimistic

- Strong communicator

- Conceptual thinker

- Can work collaboratively and independently

- High attention to detail

- Attentive listener

- Quick learner and problem solver

- Committed to the task

- Reliable and punctual

- Polite and co-operative

8. List two-three references including their name, job title, company they work for and contact details such as their phone number and email.

   Ideally you want to list people that you have worked under specifically in the design industry, so that they can vouch for your skills, abilities, work ethic and creativity. If you don't have any references in the design industry then make sure you list people that can vouch for your work ethic and skills in general that may still be relevant to the job you are applying for.

   IMPORTANT: Make sure you let the references know that you have included them on your resume and always inform them of any jobs that you have applied for so that they are prepared if they are contacted.

9. End the last page somewhere toward the bottom, with "Please visit <your website URL> to view my complete portfolio."

HOT TIP: You can even upload that PDF file to your own domain server and have that resume URL link handy to share if your PDF email attachment bounces back.

PART 4: NETWORKING

Networking is purely about building relationships and is by far the most effective job search tool you can use. It's the answer to the most common challenge students and graduates face. Too often I hear: "No one ever tells you how hard it is to actually get a job in the design industry. You're required to have experience to get a job, but you need a job to get experience."

Just like driving a car for the very first time, someone handed you the keys, trusted you and gave you a chance. They knew full well you would be nervous and a little slow to get going. Still, you've built enough rapport with this person for them to give you a shot. This is exactly like getting a job, especially if it's your first design job. I must point out though, that no matter how talented, smart or creative you are, the fact is, you aren't moving forward as fast and as effectively as the person who knows the right people.

PEOPLE ARE OPPORTUNITIES

There's a chance to meet new people everywhere you go. Whether it be the person in front of you as you wait in line at your local cafe, some of the regular people you see at the gym or friends of friends you meet at a social gathering. Each may be a link to a potential employer or even a potential personal client. Going to industry events are one way, but try not to limit yourself to that one source.

NETWORKING VIA EMAILS

I've found that sending emails are the most effective way to get an interview that will ultimately lead to a job. The thing is, once you have your online portfolio website that's easy to use, uncluttered and contains your best work, it really will speak for itself. Pair that up with your resume PDF attachment and you're really cooking with gas!

The key then is to write a personalised email that's honest, short, humble and engaging enough to cause a response. Remember the people you're writing this to are likely to be Creative Directors, Traffic or Studio Managers, HR Managers and even Managing Directors. These people will get hundreds of emails daily from others in the same boat and of course the usual day-to-day emails. They may easily miss your email or ignore it. The challenge is creating enough cut through to be heard. So how do you be different in a world full of noise?

It all comes down to storytelling.

There's no-one else like you on the planet, and besides, everyone else is taken. Everything you've become at this very moment is the sum of your experiences and learning. Embrace it, leverage it and share it. Your storytelling will achieve two important outcomes:

1. You'll create an emotional connection

2. You'll be remembered

Try not to think of storytelling as a huge task, but rather as revealing snippets of your personality that you weave into conversations. Use this approach in both written and verbal communication.

Keep your email short and direct. The person receiving it is likely to be so busy that they may only half read it. Here is an example of a letter you could write in an email that uses the approach described above:

SUBJECT LINE: OPPORTUNITIES

"Dear Vince,

I know your time is precious so I'll keep this brief.

After recently returning to Sydney from a short holiday in New York, I was happy to come home inspired and recharged. On my way home, I was greeted by some impressive branding work for Redfern plastered over suburban street banners and bus shelters, which I later found out was the work of you and your team at Frost* Collective. I feel it's a genuine symbol, providing locals and residents with the tools to address misconceptions and empower them.

My name is Ram Castillo, an up-and-coming Designer and long time fan. I recently graduated from my Advanced Diploma of Graphic Design at Billy Blue Design College (one month ago) and am hungry to get my foot in the door. After my three month internship at 'X' in Surry Hills and working part-time for a printing company over the last year, on top of some freelance jobs, I'm excited to dive into a full-time role.

If I may make a simple request that you take a look at my resume PDF attached and online portfolio: www.ramcastillo.com

I do hope that my work speaks for itself, even though I have a huge journey of learning still ahead of me. It would be an honour to work with you and your team should a Junior Design role become available. If nothing else, it would be

great to meet with you to get your advice on ways I could
improve my resume and portfolio.

I look forward to hearing from you and truly appreciate your
time.

Regards,
Ram Castillo
Designer
Mobile: XXX XXX
www.ramcastillo.com"

Whatever you decide to write in your email on your job
search, the anatomy of it should look like this:

1. Subject line should be short, relevant and appealing

2. Salutation

3. Acknowledge their superiority and state time constraint

4. A very short personal experience that links you to them

5. Your reason for writing, backed up with high value claims
   such as achievements

6. Lead them to your work

7. Reaffirm the purpose of your writing to them with more
   specificity

8. Sign off with your contact details

Writing with some heart and soul will always resonate with people no matter who they are. Don't be afraid to put a piece of you in your email and in any interaction when networking. When you write to someone who could be a potential employer, write as if you've really put some time, thought and effort into what you're saying. Write sincerely and personalise your letter. Make them feel special. You're not the same as most job hunters who will copy and paste the same email to hundreds of employers and wonder why they don't get a response. Make receiving your email the best part of their day.

WHY YOU SHOULD MAKE LINKEDIN YOUR NEW BEST FRIEND

If you're not already a member, sign up at LinkedIn.com for free and connect with every professional you know; from your colleagues past and present, relatives to friends and even your parents' friends. Think of LinkedIn as Facebook for professionals. It's your online resume for the world to see. Keep your information up to date as it's viewable in an instant. You will also end up using this to message influential people directly for any opportunities anytime you like. The bonus is they'll also be able to reach you or may even stumble upon your profile.

After you've completed your profile, which is well worth the time and effort, start adding people to your network. You can even try to 'connect' (add to your network) with people you haven't formally met with directly. They'll need to approve your 'connect' request, so when you put your reason for knowing them, just be honest by filling in the personal note box. This is important. This in my opinion makes all the difference, especially if you don't actually know them in person. An example would be: "Hi Michael, we haven't formally met yet but I just stumbled across your work and thought I'd connect with you here on LinkedIn" or "Hi Michael, we haven't formally met yet but I just read your article on your company's blog and thought I'd connect with you here on LinkedIn." Keep it short and light-hearted. You don't want to be screaming 'give me a job' when you haven't even passed the gates yet.

In my opinion the top four key features of LinkedIn in order are:

1. **The search tool:** you can search for people, jobs and companies. Contacting people in this one portal makes networking easy.

2. **Newsfeed:** besides keeping up to date with articles and thoughts from industry peers, you'll occasionally have people in your network posting job roles. As the saying goes, "It's not what you know, but who you know". For the most part, I do feel this definitely has merit. Especially when an average of about 80-85% of jobs in western countries are filled through referrals and 'word of mouth'. Only about 15-20% of jobs available are publicly advertised. I'd like to think a more accurate quote is, "It's not about who you know, it's about who knows you".

3. **Recommendations and endorsements from industry peers**: this adds powerful credibility, social proof and believability of who you are, what you've delivered and what you're capable of.

4. **A completed profile:** this is your online resume and is a huge part of your online presence and personal brand.

WOULD YOU SWIM ALONE WITH SHARKS? NOT HAVING A CAREER MENTOR IS EXACTLY THAT

If you were a child and had severe asthma, and absolutely loved soccer, but found it 'too hard' to play a full game, would you give up and just play FIFA 2013 on Xbox? (Don't answer that, it's actually really addictive). Honestly, would you think it was impossible to become a professional soccer player with such a terrible respiratory condition? Well, David Beckham didn't. Arguably one of the greatest soccer players in the world, David still has it and has suffered with this since he was a young boy (Daily Mail UK, 2009).

This didn't stop him from playing 65 games a season for over 20 years and winning countless world class trophies.

Bobby Charlton was his mentor. A former English football player, regarded as one of the greatest midfielders of all time and considered the greatest English player of all time.

—

MENTORING IS A TIMELESS PHENOMENON THAT HAS PROVIDED A SPRINGBOARD FOR CAREER SUCCESS FOR MANY.

— LEGACY AND LEGACY

—

In recent times, one can point to not only David Beckham, but Richard Branson, Michael Jackson, Mike Tyson, Roger Federer, Eminem and Nelson Mandela as notable icons, all of whom have benefited from the investment of a mentor.

A career mentor is a person that acts as an adviser, a motivator, a counsellor, and a guiding force in your career. This person should have relevant industry experience and should be a professional whom you can talk openly with and from whom you can expect to receive sound, unbiased career advice.

Traditionally, mentoring is something that you would not purchase and would not require a monetary exchange. The relationship between a mentor and a person being mentored is far higher than what money can buy.

HOW DOES THIS AFFECT MY DESIGN CAREER?

Take a look at these proven positive statistics:

Retention

- 77% of companies report that mentoring programs were effective in increasing retention
- Turnover reductions of 20% with mentoring
- 35% of employees who do not receive regular mentoring look for another job within 12 months

Promotion

- 75% of executives point to mentoring as playing a key role in their careers

- 70% of women of colour who had a mentor received a promotion

- The more mentors a woman had, the faster she moved up the corporate ladder

Productivity

- Managerial productivity increased by 88% when mentoring was involved, versus only a 24% increase with training alone

- 95% of mentoring participants said the experience motivated them to do their very best

Personal and Professional Development

- More than 60% of college and graduate students listed mentoring as a criterion for selecting an employer after graduation

- 35% of CFOs said the single greatest benefit of working with a mentor was having a confidant and advisor

- Professionals who have had mentors earn between $5,610 and $22,450 more annually than those who have not

WHAT ARE THE BENEFITS OF HAVING A CAREER MENTOR?

A career mentor is invaluable because they are there to support and guide you and answer any questions that as a beginner you may have. There are many benefits to having a mentor, including those that follow:

- Individual recognition, encouragement, and support
- Increased self-esteem and confidence when dealing with professionals
- Increased confidence to challenge oneself to achieve new goals and explore alternatives
- A realistic perspective of the workplace
- Advice on how to balance work and other responsibilities and set priorities
- Knowledge of workplace 'dos and don'ts'
- Experience in networking
- Increase in technical knowledge
- Further development of career potential
- Personal development

A GOOD CAREER MENTOR

- Provides relevant industry-related perspectives
- Is committed to the mentoring relationship
- Is respectful of you as an individual

- Is a good listener

- Does not judge your difference of opinion

- Is sensitive to your struggle

- Is stable and flexible

- Is honest, patient and trustworthy

SWEET, HOW DO I FIND A GOOD CAREER MENTOR?

- Define the attributes and characteristics of the designer you want to be

- Find experts who are doing what you ultimately want to become

- Look local and global (it could be your businessman father or the Creative Director of your favourite design studio – find a way to get the conversation going)

- Use whatever means necessary; phone, email, Google, LinkedIn, Behance, Twitter, Facebook, anything and everything

- Show your potential both through your work, your achievements and how you spend your time. Mentors will only choose to invest their time with you if they feel you are optimistic, humble yet enthusiastic, hungry to learn and willing to take action.

- Once you have made friendly contact explaining your objectives, if they are interested, discuss what arrangement would work for them. Face-to-face would be ideal, but not a hindrance if it's not possible. It could be a simple conversation once a week over the phone for an agreed amount of time, it could be over email, it could even be over a set Skype meeting

- Don't limit yourself to one or two mentors, you should have as many as you think will benefit you. Some mentors will be great for certain areas and others may have a broader offering

WHAT DO MENTORS GET OUT OF IT?

- The satisfaction of helping a student reach their academic and professional goals

- A chance to be inspired and engaged by young talent with a passionate personality

- Recognition at work for participation in a job-related volunteer activity

- An expanded network of professional colleagues

- Recognition for service to the community

- Increased self-esteem, self-confidence and affirmation of professional competence

—

Not having a good mentor is costing you dearly. Without their guidance and experience, you are going to have to start at the very beginning and make all the mistakes yourself.

– Jonny Gibaud

—

You wouldn't go swimming alone with sharks, so don't do it in the work force. You would do your research first right? And surround yourself with a team of people that know what they're doing.

So no matter how much research you do, you'll soon find out that the best way to do it is to speak to someone who has done it before. Ideally someone with quality experience and someone who can provide you with advice on the best approaches for what you are looking to achieve.

References:

http://www.lovethesepics.com/2012/08/predators-prowling-the-sea-scary-or-stunning-sharks-are-jawesome-60-pics10-vids/

http://www.3creek.com/booklets/BenefitsBooklet.pdf

http://www.dailymail.co.uk/tvshowbiz/article-1230404/David-Beckhams-biggest-secret-revealed-star-admits-Asthma.html

http://www.legacyandlegacy.com.gh/

http://www.streetdirectory.com/travel_guide/188975/careers_and_job_hunting/the_advantages_of_having_a_career_mentor.html

http://www.shesaboss.org/1st100-mentor-match-program/

http://www.nae.edu/File.aspx?id=14491

http://thelifething.com/personal-development/why-not-having-a-mentor-is-costing-you-very-dearly-indeed-and-how-to-track-a-good-one-down/

http://women2.com/2011/10/26/women-and-mentoring-in-the-united-states-linkedin-infographic/

—

DOUBTS INVADE THE MIND WHEN NOTHING ELSE FILLS IT.

– TIMOTHY FERRISS

—

PART 5: INTERVIEWS

So you've scored an interview and it's usually in a few days time. Your mind is probably going a million miles an hour, especially if you haven't had much interview experience in the past. It's natural to be nervous. This is a good thing. It's your body telling you that this is a special moment and it means something to you. Embrace it and use it to focus your energy on how badly you want the job.

Needless to say, you're probably one of five to ten people they are interviewing for the role, after reviewing hundreds of applicants. The reality is, you've made it this far so congratulations! They saw something in your portfolio and resume that they liked. They're curious to know more, so if they believe in you enough to spend some one on one time with you, then so should you. Show them who you are. Believe in your abilities and your potential.

WHAT A TWO YEAR OLD TAUGHT ME ABOUT INTERVIEWS

Secretly trapped in a two year old's body is an expert
interviewer. If you don't believe me, find one (preferably from
parents you know) and smile at them. Did they smile back
or did they not make eye contact with you at all? Try again,
perhaps stand right in front of them. Careful! You might scare
them. Maybe smile and say hello in a calm voice. Better?
Or did you make them cry?

You see two year olds are smart creatures, c'mon we've
all been there. They need to be engaged. It's not enough
to grin or nod. You've even tried to dance, make absurd
noises and play hide-and-seek with your own palms to win
their attention. This is exactly like an interview situation
except there are ways to communicate without looking
like a desperate clown.

BODY LANGUAGE

We need to acknowledge that whatever we want to have we
first need to give. If we want respect, we first need to give
respect. If we want loyalty we need to first give loyalty.
You get the idea.

So if you are giving off nervousness and uncertainty during
your interview then chances are you will also have those
same feelings reflected back at you.

―

As children, we were masters of body language. As we got older, and verbal communication increased, we lost much of our ability to use nonverbal communication to our advantage.

– Beverley Samuel

―

Look at your body as a 30 piece orchestra and the song it creates is the message you're projecting. Each have different parts to play and at different times. You can choose to use a subtle instrument or at times a group to build anticipation and intrigue. At the end of your performance, you should have strung together a captivating and harmonious demonstration of charm, talent and committed work ethic. Aim high. You'll know when you receive that standing ovation.

TONE OF VOICE

High pitched 'ums', extended 'ahs' and frequent 'I dunnos' are just some of the vehicles that carry unnecessary tone.

When responding in conversation to a potential employer, I suggest speaking as if you already know them. This thought alone has destroyed any anxiety I had before interviews. Your tone then becomes confident and relaxed.

Being down to earth is a huge box many candidates don't tick. While you're thinking, "I'm going to impress the pants out of this Director" they're thinking, "Do I really want to spend eight-ten hours of my day, five days a week with this person?"

―

One study at UCLA indicated that up to 93 percent of communication effectiveness is determined by nonverbal cues. Another study indicated that the impact of a performance was determined 7 percent by the words used, 38 percent by voice quality, and 55 percent by the nonverbal communication.

– Susan M. Heathfield

―

How to be in the zone

The night before the interview, have your portfolio ready, whether it be your pre-loaded website, a PDF on your laptop or images on your iPad. Check that it's all there and practice role playing as if you're talking through each project. Be guided by what the brief was, the challenges and the conceptual process involved that allowed you to reach those design solutions. Try to get your eight hours of sleep and have a high protein breakfast in the morning with plenty of water through the day to keep your mind sharp and your body energised.

HOT TIP: Eating some oats or whole-wheat toast with an omelette and a freshly squeezed juice always does the trick for me!

Aim to be 20 minutes early to the interview area. Hang around nearby, and for ten minutes just meditate, take deep breaths and start to envision the best possible outcome of the interview. Run through positive affirmations in your mind and feel it through your body. Notice your posture. Sit tall, upright and confidently. No slouching or crossing of your arms. Start to visualise a smooth and relaxed situation. Picture yourself holding pleasant eye contact and using appropriate facial expressions and hand gestures to add depth to your responses.

Remember that up to 93 percent of communication effectiveness is determined by nonverbal cues.

Think of the person interviewing you as a mirror. If you look uncomfortable and nervous then so will they. Once you've anchored your mind and body in a positive state, proceed to the interview about ten minutes early.

As you walk into the agency or studio, you'll most likely be asked to take a seat as the person interviewing you comes and meets you. Whoever it is, be it the Creative Director, Managing Director or Traffic Manager, the most important thing you need to keep on your radar is creating an emotional connection; make that connection your true north, your guide, from the start right through to the end.

Side note: There's a chance that the interviewer may be 10-20 minutes late. While it's not ideal, it does happen, but it's no reflection on you. It's simply the case that senior people often book themselves into more appointments than they really have time for, so they can run over time. However, while some people will not feel remorse of any kind for running late, other employers will be embarrassed and may therefore give you even more time and attention than they'd planned. So having someone run really late can actually be a benefit for anyone being interviewed.

WHAT DO I MEAN BY 'CREATE AN EMOTIONAL CONNECTION'?

As mentioned in the networking section of this book under 'Sending Emails', it simply means storytelling. If you meet an interesting person, you don't get that perception of them by them saying to you, "I'm interesting" and you immediately believing them. You get that impression by them talking about interesting things with their thoughts, ideas and stories. This very dynamic everyday conversation is exactly the same energy and interaction you need to transfer to the interview situation.

Practical tips to consider

- Breathe (get the blood flowing so you can think clearly)

- Smile (not the creepy kind, think George Clooney or Julia Roberts; professional yet warm and pleasant)

- Relax your shoulders

- Never fold your arms

- Avoid slouching

- Hold eye contact

- Nod when appropriate

- Add depth and character to your tone of voice

- Use the subtleties of facial expressions to add to your stories

- Take advantage of hand gesturing to create emotion

FOUR THINGS TO REMEMBER

1. Non-verbal communication improves with practice

2. You're already brilliant, continue to be better

3. There's only one of you

4. Interviews work both ways, it's also an opportunity to see if they're a good fit for you and your personal life goals

WHY YOUR ATTITUDE IS MORE IMPORTANT THAN SKILL

Compare the two following scenarios:

Common interaction between Brad (employer/interviewer) and James (job applicant/interviewee):

BRAD: "Hi James, Brad here, thanks for coming in to meet me. How are you?"

Hand shake

JAMES: "Hi Brad, pleasure to meet you, I'm good thanks."

BRAD: "Great, well we'll just take a seat in the meeting room ... so tell me James, what have you been up to recently?"

JAMES: "Just looking for work and I've had a few interviews, I've been doing a few projects on the side but that's about it."

BRAD: "Fantastic, well as you know James we're looking for a Junior Designer to work collaboratively with the team across both print, digital and experiential disciplines. Before we go through your portfolio, do you mind telling me a little about yourself and your passions?"

JAMES: "Um ... nothing much really. I work a few days a week at my local cafe and have been for the last three years. Since graduating four months ago, I've had a few freelance jobs here and there but nothing too concrete. I like to hangout with friends and go to the beach. That's about it."

BRAD: "Nice one, my favourite area is the Northern Beaches. Love it there! So let's take a look at your work and you can tell me a bit about it."

Improved interaction between Brad (employer/ interviewer) and Jake (job applicant/interviewee):

BRAD: "Hi Jake, Brad here, thanks for coming in to meet me. How are you?"

Hand shake

JAKE: "Hi Brad, nice to finally put a face to the name, I'm great thanks – very funky place you have here, I'm loving the skateboard installation on the wall!"

BRAD: "Yeah it really brings the place to life! We actually commissioned a local artist to do it. Follow me this way and we'll just take a seat in the meeting room ... so tell me Jake, what have you been up to recently?"

JAKE: "I've been fairly busy, after graduating four months ago, I took two months off to go backpacking in Europe and ticked off three things on my bucket list! One was hang gliding in Switzerland, the second was seeing Gaudí's Sagrada Familia in Barcelona in person and the third was to eat frogs' legs in Paris. Since coming back, I've been going to industry events, networking and trying my best to find a Junior Design role at a place I can contribute to with passionate people I can learn from."

BRAD: "That's really refreshing to hear as we need more people with your enthusiasm and energy! Well as you know Jake we're looking to fill a Junior Designer role to work collaboratively with the team across both print, digital and experiential disciplines. Before we go through your portfolio, do you mind telling me a little more about yourself and your passions?"

JAKE: "Of course. Well, I think that I owe a lot of my journey so far to my parents. They led with their actions, instilled strong values in me and allowed me to dream. I remember when I was seven, I drew all over the wall with crayon, and my mother said calmly that I could finish my drawing but I had to clean it up after! They were respectful and hard working. Something I wish to bring to the table no matter where I work. On top of my design talent I hope!"

BRAD: "Haha you're lucky to have parents like that! It just shows how important it is to have that support network at a young age and be able to appreciate that now. Okay, so let's take a look at your work and you can tell me a bit about each piece as you flick through it."

It may not seem like a huge difference but what's in between the lines is attitude and that's the spark they're after. Take James for instance who took more of a backseat approach while Jake was more proactive and took advantage of the open questions by sharing his journey. When that level of storytelling is shared, as Jake did, and continues throughout a whole interview with confident posture, natural facial expression, tone and appropriate hand gestures, it'll project an enthusiastic and positive energy.

The facts are, it's highly likely the employer interviewing you has already assessed your work and resume. They're actually meeting you in person to get to know your attitude, your work ethic and your values. Skill is something that they'll assume you're already competent with or something they feel you can learn. Employers know you can master skill quite quickly through repetition.

Attitude on the other hand stems from values, belief systems and personal rules. It's not so easily taught and it is really about a person's concrete way of thinking or feeling, typically reflected in their behaviour. You may already know the importance of this, but is it part of your character? Most of the time it's a simple case of having an open mind, taking a step back and seeing the bigger picture. A small shift in perspective like this will not only have employers drawn to you, but you will begin to love challenges and have more energy in your approaches.

HOW TO BE READY FOR ANY INTERVIEW QUESTION

Now that we've established the importance of storytelling and attitude, in my experience, there are only three questions you should focus on and prepare for. The majority of the interview questions will tie back to these three. The advantage of preparing for these three umbrella questions means that you can answer most questions more naturally, by steering your answers in these three areas (Marr, 2014).

Any interviewer will want to ask questions related to these three main areas:

1. Do you have the experience, skills and expertise to undertake the role?

2. Do you have the enthusiasm and genuine interest in the role and the agency?

3. Are you going to fit into the agency's culture and team?

Don't be surprised if the interviewer varies questions and asks from different angles to get to the answers. Sometimes the interviewer won't get what he or she wants from a question, so may ask you in a different way.

Here's what's behind these three questions:

1. Do you have the experience, skills and expertise to undertake the role?

Keep your answers relevant and don't get sidetracked. The aim is to demonstrate that you're aware of the required experience, skills and expertise necessary to perform the role and that you have what it takes to deliver. They want to know your level of competence. Allow your achievements to highlight your qualities instead of merely spelling them out. When reflecting upon experiences, do so with humility and gratitude with words like: "I was fortunate enough to ..." or "I was grateful when ..." and touch upon the importance of the role that family plays, the importance of learning something new everyday and constantly being challenged. Give examples by storytelling.

Word your 'weaknesses' in a way that highlight your hunger for further knowledge and experience, for instance: "I haven't yet been fortunate enough to lead a project or a team on my own, therefore I find that my leadership skills are lacking a little but I would cherish the opportunity."

Some questions that you should expect are:

- Tell me about yourself?

- What are your greatest strengths / weaknesses?

- What can you do for us that other candidates can't?

- Why do you think you are right for this job?

- What do you think the main challenges will be?

2. Do you have the enthusiasm and genuine interest in the role and the agency?

Doing your homework can go a long way. Demonstrate that you have researched the company, understand their philosophy, specialty, current performance, structure and market position. This knowledge will show them that you can't wait to join them. I'd encourage you to consider mentioning your goals and ambitions and how they fit into the role you're applying for.

Use these insights for answering questions such as:

- What do you know about our agency?

- What do you think our agency is aiming to achieve?

- What do you know about our products and services?

- Why do you want to work for this agency?

- Why do you think this job is right for you?

- What motivates you?

3. Are you going to fit into the agency's culture and team?

This final key question is about your personality and character and how well you may fit into the team and culture of the agency. Agencies have different cultures, which translate into different ways of behaving and working. However, the relationship is both ways. Remember that you might not fit their culture and they might not fit yours. Your research on the agency will help you decide. Sometimes, it can be tricky to find detailed knowledge about the agency's culture, in which case you simply talk about your assumptions and why you feel you fit in. You want to map the culture of the agency or the team you're planning to join and compare this to your personality traits, style and behaviours.

Once you have done this you can use it to answer questions like:

- How would you describe your work style?

- How would you describe yourself?

- How would your colleagues describe you?

- What makes you a good fit for our agency?

- What makes you a good team member?

- If you were an animal, what animal would you be?

All interviews are a two-way process. In the same way the interviewer wants to find out that you are right for the agency, you need to assess whether the agency is right for you.

EACH OF THE QUESTIONS CAN ALSO BE TURNED AROUND TO HELP YOU MAKE THE RIGHT DECISION:

1. By joining this agency, will I be making the most of my current skills and expertise and will they help me to grow them further?

2. Is the agency excited about having me work for them and will they provide me with the necessary support?

3. Is the agency's culture the right fit for me so that I can thrive and still be myself?

If you ask relevant questions from your point of view then this will make the interview more balanced and create a more natural conversation.

When the interview is finished, exit the interview as you entered, with gratitude and respect. Shake their hand and tell them 'thank you' and express how you've appreciated their time.

It's a win-win situation no matter what the result. At the very least, you've had interview practice and expanded your network. You've learnt something new, which you can apply and improve on for future interviews. You may get a call back for a second interview, or even a third. You may get a call offering you the job or no call at all. If you don't get a call or email back within three days, follow them up (especially if you have another offer on the table and need to make a quick decision).

Reference

Marr, Bernard, 2014, 'Job Interview: Why Only 3 Questions Really Matter',
http://linkd.in/1qmt3cC

WHAT TO DO WHEN YOU GET A JOB OFFER

It's very easy to accept the first offer that comes along, especially when the design industry continues to be increasingly competitive. The natural reaction is to leap onto the offer right away. But before you do, consider the following:

1. **Is the salary being offered industry standard for your role and experience?**

The best way to find this figure is to do some research online on websites from reputable organisations and to ask industry peers and mentors. It of course depends on what country you're from to find an accurate median figure, however the key websites that I would suggest you take a look at are: www.coroflot.com/designsalaryguide (covers a variety of countries), www.designsalaries.aiga.org (covers the American market) and www.glassdoor.com.au (transparent data from companies and employees worldwide).

—

*Learn to use your creative insights
to your advantage at the bargaining table.*

*Creatives are vastly under paid in our society. Think about it, the
world around us was conceived and built by intuitive, creative
people. Yet in major cities, lawyers are paid five times what
creatives are paid, on average. Why? Because lawyers are much
more comfortable asking for the money than we are.*

*It's a dilemma that stems from deep in our creative roots. Creatives
are more in touch with their feelings than the general population.
Our vulnerabilities are closer to the surface. Those vulnerabilities
can burden us with uncomfortable feelings and unwanted physical
reactions when we are under the stress brought on by negotiation.
The very sensitivities that designers use to make their work
connect on an emotional level are a liability at the bargaining table.
They are a liability unless we learn to expect those feelings and use
our sensitivities to understand what's going on, to guide our steps
and our intuitions. Then our insights and intuitions can become a
powerful advantage.*

— Ted Leonhardt, Author: Nail It, Stories for Designers on
Negotiating with Confidence.

—

2. Do you have any other offers on the table that you can leverage against the other in terms of salary?

Of course salary is only one factor when accepting a job offer. The currency of experience, working with great talent and enjoying the agency's culture are also huge factors. However, I'm a big believer in the power of asking questions. If you don't ask, the answer will always be no. Besides, you have nothing to lose and everything to gain. Try it and see. If you're ever in this situation, ask agency 'A' something to this effect: "Thank you so much for the offer, I'm quite torn because I've also been offered the same role at another agency with a salary that's $10K more than your offer. I am more drawn to your agency as I feel it's a better fit, but that salary difference will go a long way, especially with the high cost of living in the area. I would love it if you could match it?" Even if agency 'A' can only increase it by half of what the difference is, it's still an increase nonetheless.

3. Do you have any other interviews coming up that you'd like to attend first in case they make an offer?

In which case, ask if you could take a day or two to think about the offer, but reaffirm that you're incredibly interested. If they probe further, simply tell them the truth. That you have a few interviews lined up over the next few days and feel that in order to commit 100% you'd like to give the other interviews a good go as well, as you feel this is what's fair for yourself and the agency you end up joining.

Not accepting the offer right away is a good thing. It takes guts but it shows that you respect yourself enough to think through an important decision. I'm by no means encouraging you to 'play hard to get' for amusement's sake. If you're as sure as you can be and the first offer you get is exactly what you want then definitely accept. If you feel unsure, then do consider the above.

At the end of the day, when there are challenging decisions to be made, ask yourself:

"Which will I regret the most?" Therein lies your answer.

—

I have always been asked by a multitude of people and organisations, what is the secret to putting together awesome teams that have to operate on the edge of chaos?

I say edge of chaos because those that really understand what it takes to make a difference also realise that the best talent that brings innovation and creativity do in fact operate on the edge of chaos. Therein lays the challenge since this same talent is faced with a environment that ultimately is run by the need to make profit and more often than not is risk averse.

So what does this mean? It means that if you are going to make an impact on the executive (the Directors, the VPs, those with budget authority) that will either unleash you or kick you to the curb, you need to quantify things in their world and in their language.

Deliver your message in terms they can quantify, qualify and is wrapped in their core values. Do all that and have a manager that can navigate the executive landscape and magic will occur.

Remember it's not your talent, it's the rules of the game that can hold you back. So don't foul out even before you start!

– Bane Hunter CEO of The Loop (theloop.com.au) and board member of Blue Chilli (bluechilli.com)

—

SUMMARY

1. Your design thinking and execution must be relevant, single-minded, intelligent and creative to the brief or task. All the while encompassing a sense of imagination.

2. You must show your personal brand in its best light at every touch point. From your portfolio, to your online presence to your face-to-face interviews. Project your core values, such as: confidence, humility, gratitude, enthusiasm and patience.

3. You should learn to be personable. Meet people wherever you go and expand your network. Leverage the online space to reach industry peers and leaders. Use your storytelling skills whenever you get the chance to create an emotional connection and be memorable to those you are interacting with.

4. Ask plenty of questions. Explore, investigate, interrogate and be curious.

5. If you stay hungry for continuous learning, you will see adventure, feel satisfaction and taste reward no matter what the situation or circumstance.

—

I ALWAYS WONDER WHY BIRDS CHOOSE TO STAY IN THE SAME PLACE WHEN THEY CAN FLY ANYWHERE ON THE EARTH, THEN I ASK MYSELF THE SAME QUESTION.

— HARUN YAHYA

—

PARTING WORDS

Remember at the beginning of this book, I mentioned that on my solo backpacking adventures in Europe for five months, something in particular happened? Something magical and memorable?

Well, one particular rainy afternoon when I was in Barcelona, Spain, I got lost. No map, no idea. I embraced the spontaneity and made my way through the cobblestoned streets. Eventually, I stopped at a small, almost hidden tapas and drinks bar that whispered days of old. When I entered, I felt a sense of warmth and tranquility. The place smelt of Mum's home cooking mixed with red wine and cigars. All you could hear was the soft jazz music coming out of the tiny ancient speaker. I was the only customer. The old bearded man that greeted me was the owner. He was relaxed, friendly, moved a little slowly and spoke reasonably good English. He asked if I wanted something to eat or drink. I said, "Both would be great," as I sat on the bar stool. We made our introductions and got talking about the world, and cigars. He really liked his cigars. As he offered me one from a beautiful wooden chest (that made me question if my bill was going to increase through the roof beyond my 12 euro paella), I joined him for his daily ritual.

Behind the minimal selection of 1980s scotch, I noticed three framed black and white photographs. One with him and what looked like his brother. Another with him and who I assumed to be his wife. And the third with him and what looked like his children. When I asked who they were, he paused and just smiled. Not of the joyful kind, more of the nostalgic, mysteriously sad kind. He then redirected the conversation back to me and asked me what the purpose of my travels was. I gave him the same response, a poor excuse for a smile and silence like a log.

He then slid a scrap piece of paper and a black pen over the counter and said, "Write down one specific thing that would make you happy and date it."

What I wrote down is actually in your hands right now. A bunch of words that raced through your eyes and hopefully into your mind.

The following page shows a photo of that exact piece of paper.

Too often we get trapped in a world that's so fast, we forget that our dreams are as real as we're committed to making them.

That life is simple if we just decide.

All that's left now, is for you to do.

28 July, 2009

To write a book
that helps people.

ACKNOWLEDGEMENTS

As my first ever published book, I'd like to make some acknowledgements to those that contributed to helping bring this idea to life in some shape or form. You've allowed me to live my dream. Thank you with all my heart.

God: Without you, I would be nothing. I owe you everything.

Mum and Dad: I hope to pass the same seeds of love you have planted in me to everyone I meet. Thank you for teaching me that in order to have, one must first give.

My brother Ryan and sister Raisa: You are true examples of loyalty and friendship. I love you both dearly.

Lola Carol Santos: You are actually superwoman and are living proof of being as young as you feel.

Vivian Tham: My rock and my 24/7 soundboard. My advisor, my biggest supporter and my partner in crime. You create the harmony on this journey worth playing to.

Ian Wingrove: You're the best mentor anyone could ever ask for. I'm forever grateful for this, your guidance and your friendship. Both as a Creative Director and a leader. Thank you for giving me a chance to shine.

Scott Stephenson: Look where your suggestion to start a blog has taken me. Our conversations make this crazy world so simple. Let's never forget it.

Jason Seblain: You make time for what matters and tell it how it is with such few words. You deserve every avalanche of success because of your true generosity.

Matthew Prain: Mr. Optimism, your adventures are a testament to your infectious love for life and I'm glad to be a part of it.

Marie Ramos: You're a needle in a wheat field. Constantly inspiring the uninspired without even knowing it. The universe is no doubt smiling upon you.

Matt Eastwood, Ben Lilley, Scott Smith, Andrew Hoyne, Ian Wingrove, Daniel Farrugia, Marco Eychenne, Declan Mimnagh, Ted Leonhardt, Grant Higgins, Eric Wilson, Tim Fox and **Alisha Allport** for contributing personal testimonials. Special thanks to **Bane Hunter, Vince Frost** and **Michael Schepis** too for your insights. I'm incredibly humbled and respect you all immensely.

Timothy Ferriss and **Tony Robbins**: Both need no introduction, my motivation and philosophies to take action have been built by your words in the last five years. You've both changed my life forever.

Last but certainly not the least, to all of you who have read this book. This is all for you. Be brave. Be willing to question, explore and dissect business problems on your quest for humanised creative solutions. Adapt with change. Fail, but fail quickly in order to succeed. Whatever path you choose to reach your destination, remember to want it bad, as bad as you want to breath.

RESOURCES

giantthinkers.com
A leading blog-based resource that provides real, practical and direct advice to design students and graduates on how to get a job as a designer. It encourages up and coming designers to push their own personal boundaries by empowering them with relevant and proven information to be employable.

theloop.com.au
Australia's largest professional creative community and expanding globally. It's your one stop shop for creating your online portfolio, resume, job searching, networking, study options, getting inspired and much more.

design.tutsplus.com
Tuts+ offers video courses and written tutorials to help you learn creative skills in code, design and illustration, photography, video, music, web design, game development, craft, and more. The best part is that tutorials are available to you completely free – all 16,000 of them!

lynda.com
An online learning company that helps anyone learn software, design, and business skills to achieve their personal and professional goals.

thefwa.com

Numero uno. The first and best showcase website on the entire Internet for interactive work. This should be the one site you check at least once a week for the rest of your life. See what's hot in the world of digital.

dribbble.com

An inspirational website with great designers giving viewers a snapshot of what they are working on. It's a great resource to see WIP (work in progress) of logos and designs. It's all restricted to a small window snapshot. It's a good way to see UI designs up and close too.

webcreme.com

Another great inspiration/showcase website. It is frequently updated, and it has a simple interface to scroll through. A good site to get the old brain inspired before work. (Be sure to check out Google Chrome's infinity scroll extension as well, to scroll through multiple pages at once).

pinterest.com

Pinterest is a great way to see and archive for reference/re-pin images. You can also follow your favourite designers. Build an online collection of designs that can always help you in a sticky situation.

psd.tutsplus.com

PSD tuts is part of a chain of websites that has been around for quite some time now. It was one of the first websites of an umbrella company called Envato, which helps blog resources and tutorials on anything creative related. Be sure to check out this website if you want to try something new, or its other sister websites as well.

abduzeedo.com

A great inspirational website, that covers topics like illustrations, artworks, artists, web design, print design ... Basically nearly everything. Fabio, the creator of this website, is an insanely hard worker that has built up this website to the level of fame it has today.

cssremix.com

A showcase of HTML5 and CSS websites that get featured in a showcase style of view. Since the future is heading towards more HTML5 coding for smart devices, this is a good website to see these types of work.

twitter.com

Needless to say, twitter allows you to follow your inspirations, and share your inspirations for your followers to see.

creattica.com

Another great showcase website of work. Generally shows basic designs.

mobileawesomeness.com

A good archive of mobile-friendly websites.

webdesignerwall.com

A great blog for web designers and inspiration.

behance.net

Behance. Is. Awesome. Inspiration of all creative disciplines. They also have other partner websites and the ability to specify certain creative fields such as typography, design, art direction, motion and photography.

thenounproject.com

A great resource to get high quality simplistic vector icons, from helpful icons designers that contribute their time for free. But it comes with good will in return, with attribution of course. You can either help these authors by attributing them on your designs, or contributing a small fee to use their icons into your design without mention. A good way to get designs rolling, until you can design your own.

psdcovers.com

PSD covers is a wonderful automation actions tool to be used with Photoshop, to mock up any design you please onto an in-situ shot for your designs. It's completely free, and has a massive archive of pre-setup items. All you need to do is paste, and dust your hands while the computer does your work for you.

google.com/webfonts

Google web fonts is what all digital designers should be immersed in day after day. It's a gigantic online archive, of completely free fonts provided by Google and its authors that have already been coded and prepared to be used dynamically online. Say goodbye to using only web standard fonts in headings (as images), and say hello to HTML5 and the future. Where everything is dynamic and ten times easier for your developer to create your website masterpiece into development.

smashingmagazine.com

If you're looking for more reading and less pictures, then smashing magazine is the place to be. It is one of the biggest blogs online, for design resources. 98% of my searches for resources always seem to lead me here. It has very short, straight to the point articles to help creatives find what they need. Oh, and news. It has that too.

teehanlax.com/blog

These guys are one of the best UI PSD template providers in the scene. Their PSDs are clearly organised, and they were one of the first to provide complete iOS and Android templates for digital designers to get for free. They are a digital studio as well, but their blog is great with plenty of UI resources.

365psd.com

A solid resources website, with loads of PSDs of buttons, menus and UI elements free to use.

iconfinder.com
A good resource for references of icons and icon sets.

magspreads.net
Get your magazine design fix. Magspreads is dedicated to the process and progress of magazine design and the publishing industry.

designspiration.net
A way to discover and share your design, architecture, photography and fashion inspiration. If nothing else, check out the search tool, you can't miss it.

themeforest.net
Is the world's largest marketplace for premium website themes and templates, from simple HTML to WordPress, Magento and Ghost Themes.

squarespace.com
Creative tools that help anyone give a voice to their ideas. From the designers and engineers who are creating the next generation of web and mobile experiences, to anyone putting a website together for the first time.

coroflot.com/designsalaryguide
Since 2001 Coroflot has collected and reported salary information from tens of thousands of design and creative professionals around the world.

designsalaries.aiga.org

This is the AIGA|Aquent Survey of Design Salaries and it is the most comprehensive annual survey of compensation data for the communication design profession in the United States.

glassdoor.com.au

Glassdoor holds a growing database of six million company reviews, CEO approval ratings, salary reports, interview reviews and questions, office photos and more.

To make a booking for one-on-one Skype consultations with Ram Castillo or for any enquiries, please contact ram@giantthinkers.com

If you'd like to receive free updates on topics relevant to this book, please visit giantthinkers.com for regular blog posts.

INDEX